How to Be a Breadhead

A Beginner's Guide to Baking

by Fr. Dominic Garramone, OSB

REEDY PRESS
St. Louis, Missouri

Reedy Press
PO Box 5131
St. Louis, MO 63139, USA
www.reedypress.com

Library of Congress Control Number: 2012947922

ISBN: 978-1-935806-37-0

Cover design by Bill Streeter
Interior design by Jill Halpin

Printed in the United States of America
18 19 20 21   5 4 3

Photo by Jennifer Willems, *Catholic Post*

Breadhead Course Syllabus

Breadhead Practicum

Dedicated to Jeff Elder, who first suggested a beginner's book with three basic recipes and all the variations

Lesson 1:
What Is a Breadhead?

When you hear the word "Breadhead" you might think it refers to a groupie, in the same way fans of the band the Grateful Dead are called "Deadheads," or "Parrotheads" follow Jimmy Buffett from one concert to the next. But I use the term Breadhead for an amateur who has gone from being an occasional baker to being a truly dedicated bread crafter: someone who thinks deeply about baking, who dreams about it, studies it, and arranges the family schedule to accommodate it. A Breadhead reads cookbooks the way other people read novels, keeping them stacked on the bedside table and piled up beside the comfiest chair in the living room.

In the kitchen, a Breadhead often bakes without measuring ingredients too carefully (your grandma may have been a Breadhead without knowing it) and often starts making a recipe without checking to see if all the ingredients are even in the cupboard; if not, a Breadhead finds a plausible substitution and carries on confidently. And besides, a Breadhead is never without flour and yeast on hand, because they have a permanent spot at the top of the grocery list.

Even outside the home, Breadheads maintain their enthusiasm. They discuss recipes with total strangers in grocery stores and on subway trains. On vacation, they seek out local bakeries and try to get invited into the back kitchen to see how a particular loaf is shaped. At church potlucks and bake sales, their contributions are among the first to disappear off the table, and everyone in the office is happy to see a

Breadhead colleague walk in Monday morning with something covered in plastic wrap.

Breadheads are really no different than other people with a passion for golf or scrapbooking or gardening or some other hobby. So why should you want to be a Breadhead, too?

Bread and the Web

If you are already web-savvy, you probably don't need me to tell you what to do. There are hundreds of recipe sites out there; for example, if you type "cinnamon rolls recipe" into a search engine, you'll get over 16 million suggestions (no exaggeration—try it!). But if you are Internet-challenged, I'm only going to suggest two websites. The first is my own: www.breadmonk.com. There you'll find recipes, bread baking basics, a Bread Blog, and lots more. The other site is www.homebaking.org. The purpose of the Home Baking Association is to "promote home baking by providing tools and knowledge to perpetuate generations of home bakers." Although the group is directed towards baking educators more than home bakers, you'll find lots of valuable information and links to other sites. Remember, if you have a favorite brand of flour, yeast, sugar, or any other food product, it's almost certain that the company has a website with recipes.

Lesson 2:
Why Be a Breadhead?

The Quality
Homemade bread is simply better, and often better for you, than the loaves you can get from the average grocery store, even one that has an in-store bakery. At first your loaves may not look as uniform and perfectly shaped as the ones lined up on the shelves at the local Gigantor Grocery, but the taste and texture of your homemade bread will convince you to take the time to bake and develop your skills.

The Therapy
Bread baking, as any Breadhead can tell you, is a culinary stress buster with aromatherapy thrown in, but even better since you can't eat a lighted candle. Engaging in an intentional act of creativity, especially one with vigorous physical activities like mixing and kneading, is a great way to reintegrate our fragmented selves.

The Payoff
Baking creates a tangible object that can be admired by ourselves and others, and I can testify that your neighbors, friends, and co-workers will be a lot more impressed by homemade bread than by box brownies or even cookies from scratch. A friend of mine was on maternity leave and started baking bread at home during that time. She reported that she brought both the baby and a freshly baked loaf of bread into the office, and her co-workers seemed more impressed with the bread than the baby! She said that it felt like their attitude was, "Big deal, you squeezed out a baby; we've all done that—but you *baked* this?"

The Challenge
There is a great deal of pleasure in meeting the challenge of mastering a new skill that has eluded others, even—or perhaps especially—if you have some spectacular failures along the way. I have had my share of bread disasters, and I find that developing clever and comic descriptions

of one's failures takes away the sting. Don't just use the old cliché, "You could have used my bread as a door stop." Tell people that your bread was so dense that it generated its own gravity field, or that you sent it to NASA to use in their studies of how black holes are formed. Before long everyone else will be coming up with new ways to describe your delicious loaves.

The Knowledge

I find baking rewarding because there is so much to learn about the way dough is formed: how water interacts with flour, what yeast does for the recipe, and why kneading gives the dough its lively character. Acquiring that knowledge has been a lifelong journey for me, and along the way I've encountered some great teachers: in person, on the Internet, and in books both new and old.

Look for this symbol throughout the book for suggestions for your "Breadhead Bookshelf." I must confess that I'm annoyed by cookbooks that are written as if the author invented bread baking singlehandedly! I never went to baking school (I obtained my culinary education between my mother's kitchen, PBS, and the public library), so I owe a debt of gratitude to the cookbook authors who shared their expertise, and I want my readers to learn from them, too.

The Heritage

Chances are that you have Breadheads in your family tree or traditions of baking that are important parts of your ethnic heritage. Reclaiming your bread traditions can be an immensely rewarding and meaningful pursuit. Maybe your grandmother or great-aunt was famous for making cinnamon rolls, Jewish challah, or Hungarian potato bread. Your mom or dad may have memories of a family favorite that is no longer brought to the holiday table. Reconnecting with your family history through bread could become a personal quest with emotional and spiritual rewards that go far beyond the recipes.

The Connection

Baking invites and creates community. The very word "companion" comes from the Latin *cum pane*: "with bread." A companion is someone with whom we share our bread, and the scent of bread baking will draw family members to the kitchen like nothing else. Some of my closest friendships have been formed in the kitchen: testing recipes or creating new ones, perfecting a pizza crust, or baking special breads for a party.

The Accessories

Although first-rate bread baking can be accomplished with nothing more than a bowl, a spoon, a pan, and an oven, as a Breadhead-in-Training, you'll find yourself looking longingly at stoneware crocks, special mixing tools, and heavy-duty loaf pans. If you share your wish list with family and friends, I guarantee that you will never get a crappy birthday or Christmas present again. Next we'll take a look at those baking "tools of the trade" so you'll know what you need now and what you might want later on.

Lesson 3:
Tools of the Trade

You'll want to obtain several bowls in a variety of sizes, the largest being a **five-quart mixing bowl** with high sides to keep the ingredients from escaping during mixing; many a newbie Breadhead has been put off baking because it was "just too messy." These bowls can be made of glass, glazed stoneware, or even plastic. Some bakers claim that metal bowls can create a metallic aftertaste in the dough, but I have not found this to be the case if the bowl is made of stainless steel.

Dry measuring cup, at top, and liquid measuring cup at bottom

Although a seasoned Breadhead will often add ingredients without measuring, when you're starting out accurate **measuring cups and spoons** will help to ensure your success. You'll need measuring cups for both dry and liquid ingredients, and yes, there is a difference: about 5 percent between the two. That may not seem like much, but when you're measuring out 5 or 6 cups of flour, the difference begins to add up, and you could be frustrated by a dough that is too wet or too dry. Measuring spoons are also necessary for ingredients

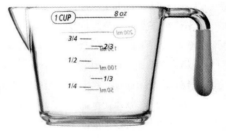

in smaller proportions, especially salt and spices. Consider spending a little more for the professional measuring spoons with long handles that can easily reach to the bottom of narrow spice jars.

If you have recipes written in the European style, a **scale** will be essential, since these recipes measure ingredients by weight rather than by volume. You'll almost certainly need one that can measure in both grams and ounces, since most European recipes use the metric system. A scale is also useful if you're trying to divide dough into even portions, like for

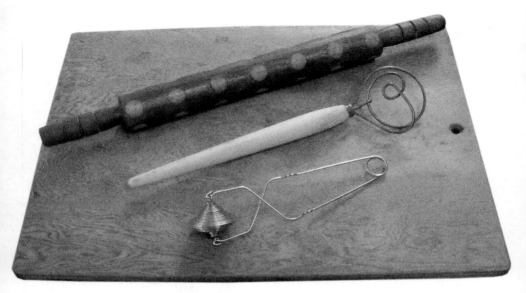

Rolling pin, dough whisk, and flour wand

perfectly uniform rolls. However, a scale is not absolutely necessary for any of the recipes in this book.

A large **wooden spoon** is the hand tool of choice for most Breadheads, and you'd be well-advised to spend a little more on a heavy-duty spoon or two. The ones that come three in a pack from the discount store just aren't sturdy enough for many doughs—I've probably broken nine or ten of them over the years! There is also an unusual mixing tool that is specific to baking called a **dough whisk** (also called a *brotpisker* by the Danish bakers who invented it). It's a heavy wooden handle with a sturdy swirl of thick wire on the end of it, and it mixes and aerates batters and doughs better than any spoon in the drawer. Put it on your birthday wish list along with those long-handled measuring spoons.

Bread dough needs to be covered during rising, so be sure to have some clean, dry **dish towels** around for that purpose. They should be made of cotton or linen weave rather than terry cloth (too much lint) and be large enough to completely cover your largest mixing bowl. (A note to quilters: If you see cotton fabric with a bread or kitchen print, buy some and make a square with a simple rolled hem, and you'll have a lovely cover for your rising dough. I have several in a variety of patterns that my quilter mother has found for me.)

For breads like cinnamon rolls or fougasse, you'll need a **rolling pin**, and the one you have in your kitchen drawer right now will work just fine, at least for most soft dough. Once you start making heavier multi-grain breads or graduate to Danish pastry, you might consider getting a wider cylindrical rolling pin without the ball-bearing handles—these allow you to push a little harder as you roll, and the wider width makes it easier to roll out larger sheets of dough.

A **pastry brush** is used to apply glazes and washes to the top of your breads, and I recommend one with soft bristles. The plastic bristle brushes are a bit too stiff and can cause an uneven surface to your loaves if you press too hard. Since some breads require spreading a soft filling like ricotta cheese or fruit preserves on a sheet of rolled out dough, a wide **spreader knife** will also prove useful, as will several sizes of **rubber spatulas**.

An **instant-read thermometer** is recommended for checking the temperature of liquids before you add the yeast. I recommend you get the electronic kind rather than one with a conventional dial, since they produce a precise temperature reading more quickly. You can also use the thermometer to test the interior temperature of a loaf of bread to ensure that it is fully baked. Baking times can vary because every oven is different with regard to air circulation and heat retention, and until you get to know your oven, a thermometer can help you avoid an underdone loaf. An **oven thermometer** that hangs on a rack inside the oven can be useful to determine if there are variations between the number on the temperature-control dial and the actual temperature inside the oven. More details on these matters are coming—stay with me!

Once the bread comes out of the oven, it should be placed on a **wire rack** to keep the bottom crust from becoming soggy as the bread cools. In a pinch, you can place fresh-baked bread on a double layer of dish towels, but even then you'll need to move the bread around as it cools to prevent moisture from collecting on the bottom. Once when I was baking in an under-equipped kitchen, I laid three wooden spoons side by side on the counter and rested my loaves on top.

A Note About Appliances

Food processors and stand mixers can be used to mix dough before shaping, and they are especially useful for potential Breadheads who have problems with carpal tunnel, arthritis, or other disabilities. However, each of these appliances has its own quirks and techniques, so you'll want to consult the instruction manuals for your appliances before using them to mix dough. The recipes in this book use the traditional method of mixing by hand. Similarly, the proportions for these recipes may not match those recommended for a bread machine.

Charles Van Over's _The Best Bread Ever: Great Homemade Bread Using your Food Processor_ (Broadway Books, 1997) is an excellent resource for those who want to use a food processor to make bread dough. I don't have any books specifically on bread making using a stand mixer, but the manufacturer's website for your model will certainly have recipes and resources for you there.

Baking Pans

To make all the recipes in this book, you will need only three different styles of pans: a **baking sheet**, a **loaf pan**, and a **muffin tin**.

Metal **baking sheets** themselves come in two styles: those with a slightly raised side (also called a jelly-roll pan) and those without sides, often used to bake cookies. For the most part you can use either of these kinds of baking sheets for the recipes in this book, but I recommend that you buy the heavy-duty variety that are non-flexible. The thin baking sheets used for cookies in most homes become warped over time, which can cause your breads to bake unevenly, and the thin metal makes the possibility of a scorched bottom crust a real danger. In a pinch, stack two of these thinner sheets together, and the layer of air between the two will prevent a burnt crust. Most bakers prefer a non-stick coating for these pans, but I've done just fine with untreated metal pans, too.

Loaf pans generally come in three sizes: small, medium, and large. The smallest pans (sometimes called mini-loaf pans) are 5¾ × 3½ × 2 inches, and are often used for gift breads. The medium-size pans are 8½ × 4½ × 2½ inches and hold about 24 ounces of dough each. The large size is 9 × 5 × 3 inches and holds up to two and a quarter pounds of dough. Most of the recipes in this book are scaled for the medium-size pans, with the exception of Pull Apart Garlic Bread, which uses the larger 9 × 5 inch pans.

You probably already have **muffin tins** in the house, especially if you have children who require cupcakes for a classroom treat or a soccer team party. If you need to shop, look for pans with a deep cup and a non-stick surface. A shallow cup makes for a stingy-looking muffin, and cleaning baked-on muffin batter out of those little cups is a real pain. I'm not a fan of paper liners, since the liner pulls off most of the outer crust of a fresh, warm muffin, which of course is an essential part of the enjoyment of the muffin!

As you progress in the Way of the Breadhead, you'll find yourself looking at stoneware pans (completely non-stick once they're conditioned properly, and they yield a terrific crust), French baguette trays, molds for pan d'oro and brioche, cast-iron segmented skillets for scones, Dutch ovens for large sourdough loaves—more items for the wish list!

In his remarkable book _The Supper of the Lamb_, Robert Capon has a recipe for bread that is mixed and baked in a single vessel: a large saucepan with a metal handle! The book has only a few recipes, but offers profound spiritual reflections on cooking, as well as a wealth of practical tips on how to choose and sharpen kitchen knives, the secret to making first-rate sauces and gravies, how puff pastry works, and other culinary mysteries.

One Last Special Tool

One of the most useful tools I have ever encountered is a **flour wand**: a tool made of wire with a squeeze handle and a spring coil on the end. It was first developed in Victorian times when pie making became especially popular. When the handle is squeezed, the spring opens up, which is then swirled in the flour container. Releasing the handle traps the flour in the coil, which is then shaken gently to sprinkle just the right amount of flour onto the countertop. If you've ever had both hands covered in raw pie crust or sticky bread dough and have been reluctant to reach into the flour canister, you'll understand why this tool is particularly valuable. They are available in some specialty shops and on several websites online.

Now that you've assembled at least the basic equipment—bowl, mixing spoon, measuring devices, and baking pans—let's take a stroll through the Breadhead pantry and see what ingredients you'll need and learn a bit about how they function in a bread recipe.

Lesson 4:
The Kinds of Flour

A wheat kernel has three basic parts: bran, germ, and endosperm. The bran is the husk that encloses the endosperm, which is rich in starch and protein. At the center of the kernel is the wheat germ, the nutritious heart of the seed that eventually grows into the new wheat plant. Various flours are formed by including or removing the parts of the wheat kernel.

Wheat can be considered "hard" or "soft" depending upon the protein content of the grain. "Hard" wheat with a higher protein content is generally grown in colder climates, while "soft" wheat is produced in milder regions and has a lower percentage of protein. Protein, as we'll learn later, is an essential part of the bread-making process, so hard wheat flours with a higher protein content are preferable for our purposes. Soft wheat flours are better for quick breads like muffins, biscuits, and pancakes.

All-purpose flour is a milled combination of hard and soft wheat grains—the bran and the germ are removed during milling, hence its whiter appearance. Many national brands also include some barley in the mix to assist with yeast production. As with many all-purpose, "one size fits all" products, it's serviceable enough, but it has too much protein for really great pie crusts and tender muffins and not quite enough for first-rate kneaded yeast breads. The recipes in this book, however, can be made with all-purpose flour (I generally use all-purpose flour because that's what the abbey kitchen manager orders!), but the end product will be superior in lightness and texture when a higher protein blend is used.

Just to complicate matters further, flour comes in **bleached** and **unbleached** forms. Bleached flour obviously gives a whiter appearance to the bread, but some people believe it also imparts something of a metallic tang to the flavor, depending upon chemicals used in the bleaching process. Because many bakers prefer an unbleached flour for their yeast breads, millers often add a little extra hard wheat to unbleached flour to give it a slightly higher percentage of protein. If you choose all-purpose flour, try to find an unbleached variety.

Bread flour is milled from harder wheat and hence has a greater percentage of the desired proteins. Because protein absorbs water more than the starch in flour, you will use a little less flour in a recipe when you use bread flour instead of all-purpose. You will want to use bread flour whenever you can, but especially for the white flour in the Basic Wheat Dough Recipe (see page 52).

Whole wheat flour has all the parts of the wheat grain—bran, endosperm, and germ—included in the flour, making for a more complex, earthier flavor and greater nutrition in the bread. However, the inclusion of the bran and the germ means that whole wheat flour has less protein by volume, so a loaf made entirely from whole wheat flour can be heavy and dense. It's usually combined with all-purpose or bread flour: Two parts bread flour to one part wheat is considered a good proportion.

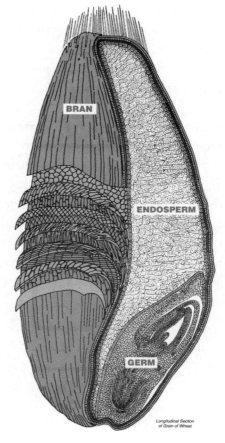

BRAN

ENDOSPERM

GERM

Longitudinal Section
of Grain of Wheat

There are some other special wheat flours like semolina and durum, and other grains like rye, oatmeal, spelt, millet, and quinoa that are added to various breads, but we'll save those for another day. All the recipes in this book can be made with the flours described above. But we're never going to get anywhere unless we talk about yeast.

Lesson 5:
Introduction to Yeast

Yeast is a microorganism that consumes the natural sugars in flour and produces alcohol and carbon dioxide in the process. The production of alcohol is what makes wine and beer possible, but it's the CO_2 that interests Breadheads, because the yeast's production of this gas causes bread dough to rise.

Like flours, yeast comes in a variety of forms. **Fresh yeast** comes in the form of a soft, crumbly cake found in the refrigerated section of many supermarkets. It has to be used within a few days of purchase as it loses its freshness rapidly, so unless you are a daily baker you will probably prefer some other form. **Active dry yeast** is more shelf stable—the package will have an expiration date—and must be activated in warm water. Active dry yeast will be used for all the recipes in this book, except in the ice cream muffins.

Fast rising yeast is found in packages similar to active dry yeast, but it comes in smaller particles and may have ascorbic acid added to speed the growth of the yeast. It is usually mixed with a portion of the flour, and then warm liquid is added. It's best to use this yeast only in recipes that call for it. **Instant yeast** is often used in commercial bakeries, and it is also stirred into a portion of the dry ingredients before adding some or all of the liquid in a recipe. It is similar to the yeast used for bread machines. Authentic **sourdough yeast** is wild yeast captured from the air. It's a different species of yeast than commercial yeast and requires an entirely different method.

The most detailed book on sourdough yeast is <u>Classic Sourdoughs, Revised: A Home Baker's Handbook</u> (Ten
Speed Press, 2011), by Ed Wood and Jean Wood. You'll find out how to capture wild yeast, how to grow sourdough starter, and how to use it to get consistent results. Sourdough starters are also available online. <u>Sourdough Jack's Cookery and Other Things</u> (Argonaut, 1972), by Jack Mabree, gives the Alaskan frontier perspective on the subject and is both informative and entertaining. It's now out of print, but I see it on eBay all the time.

The recipes in this book use active dry yeast, which most often comes in a "three-strip"—three packages of yeast connected together with perforations between. Each package holds 7 grams of yeast, or about 2¼ teaspoons. That amount of yeast is enough to raise dough using up to four cups of flour. A recipe calling for five or six cups of flour (an average amount for a two-loaf batch) will therefore require two packages of active dry yeast, but when in doubt, just follow the recipe. However, if you double the recipe, you do not double the amount of yeast. Instead, take the number of cups of flour and divide it by four. The resulting number will tell you how many packages of yeast to use. For example, a recipe that calls for six cups of flour would use two packages of yeast but when doubled would only require three packages: 12 divided by 4 equals 3.

Ooof! Didn't know you were going to get a math lesson, did you? If you haven't already abandoned me for a boxed mix of muffins with artificial blueberry bits, let's turn to something a little less strenuous and a great deal more flavorful: sugar, salt, butter, and eggs.

Lesson 6:
Other Ingredients

Liquids

The most common liquid for bread is **water**, and the kind of water you use really does make a difference. Hard water, or water that is heavily chlorinated, can inhibit yeast growth and affect the taste of the finished loaf. Some people recommend spring water for yeast breads, especially for sourdough, but I find that any filtered or purified water will do. Our monastery kitchen has a reverse osmosis filter for its drinking water, and that's what usually gives me the best results.

When **milk** is used in a recipe, it gives the bread a more tender crumb, as do other milk products like **buttermilk**, **yogurt**, or **sour cream**, which also provide additional flavor. When these last three ingredients are used, sometimes the recipe will call for the addition of a little baking soda to counteract the tangy flavor, especially in sweet breads.

Other liquids can be used to make bread. For example, **tomato juice** gives the dough a lovely salmon color and savory flavor, especially when accompanied by herbs like basil and rosemary. **Potato water** (that is, water in which potatoes have been boiled) is said to promote yeast growth and make the dough softer; mashed potatoes added to the mix have the same effect to a greater degree. There is even a bread called *pain vigneron* (winemaker's bread) that uses **red wine** as the primary liquid in the dough.

Salt

The salt in a bread recipe has several functions. It slows down the fermentation process of the yeast, which strengthens the development of gluten, the principal protein that gives bread its structure (see page 24). Bread with salt has a longer shelf life, and of course it adds flavor.

Ordinary table salt is used in all the recipes in this book, but other recipes may use kosher or sea salts of various flavors. Salt is also used as a topping for breads like pretzels and focaccia.

In the Middle Ages, Tuscany's neighboring city states controlled the salt market and taxed it heavily, and in protest the Tuscans developed saltless bread with a yeasty flavor. But since such bread stales quickly, they also became expert at developing recipes for using up stale bread! For those on a low-sodium diet, many bakers recommend reducing the amount of salt in a recipe by half, but not eliminating it altogether.

Sugars

Like salt, sugar has more than one function in bread dough. In times past, sugar was used to give additional food for the yeast, especially in the early stages of development. However, modern commercial yeasts have been carefully bred and grown so they will produce consistent, reliable results—a great boon to home and professional bakers alike—so sugar is not as necessary in modern baking, at least for the purpose of yeast development. But the various kinds of sugar used in baking also enhance the flavor and texture of bread. Granulated sugar, brown sugar, molasses, honey, and malt extract are all used to flavor bread.

Oils and Fats

Enriching ingredients like oil and butter make bread moister with a soft, tender crumb. They are not strictly necessary to make bread—Italian-style pizza dough never includes it—but the rich, cake-like texture of brioche and the soft interior of dinner rolls would be impossible without it. However, any kind of fat or oil coats the protein strands in the dough and slows the process of fermentation, so breads with a high fat content can require a much higher rising time. One way to help this problem is to add these larger amounts of fat a little later in the mixing process, after some of the flour has been mixed in or even during the kneading process. The amount of oil or butter in the recipes of this book does not require this adjustment.

Eggs

Eggs are another enriching ingredient, which also impart a more cake-like texture to bread. Make a batch of cinnamon rolls without an egg or two in the dough and you'll notice the difference, and the glorious golden color of Jewish challah is produced by a generous use of eggs as well. Most recipes, including the ones in this book, assume the use of large or extra-large chicken eggs. If you use duck or goose eggs of different sizes, you may need to make some adjustments in the amount of flour. Brushing the top of a loaf of bread with a beaten egg just before it goes in the oven produces a deep, golden-brown crust; using just the egg whites as a wash produces a crisper crust.

Herbs, Fruits, and Vegetables

Herbs, fruits, and vegetables have been used for thousands of years to enhance the flavor of bread. The archaeological and literary evidence proves that Egyptian, Greek, and Roman bakers all enhanced their breads with local produce, and every culture has been following their example ever since. Nearly every ethnic group has holiday breads adorned with fresh or dried fruits, and modern bakers have added chocolate to the ingredient list as well. I have an herb garden just outside the back door to the abbey kitchen, and our Brother Luke brings in vegetables from the monastery garden to inspire new creations throughout the summer and fall. Several of the recipes in this book were developed because of an abundance of produce in the garden or the fridge!

Okay, enough about tools and ingredients: Let's roll up our sleeves, put on an apron, and get our hands in the dough.

If you're interested in the history of bread making, be sure to check out _Six Thousand Years of Bread: Its_  _Holy and Unholy History_ (The Lyons Press; revised edition, 1997), by H. E. Jacobs, who researched the subject for decades. Jacobs follows the history of bread from its beginning in ancient Egypt and continues through to modern times, concluding with his own experiences in a Nazi concentration camp, living on bread made of sawdust. A more visual book, Bernard Dupaigne's _The History of Bread_ (Abrams, 1999) includes a wealth of historical paintings, pictures, and photos of baking throughout the centuries, accompanied by an informative text.

Lesson 7:
The Mechanics of Mixing

If you have made pancake batter from a box, you will have no trouble with the first stages of mixing bread, but later on things get a little stickier. The following instructions are repeated in later recipes in a somewhat abbreviated form; refer back to these pages if you are uncertain.

1. Assemble your equipment: bowl, mixing spoon, measuring cups and spoons, thermometer, and a clean countertop. Remove hand jewelry, and wash and dry your hands.

2. Check to make sure you have all your ingredients in sufficient amounts for the recipe (professional chefs call this the *mise en place*). Check the expiration date on the yeast packages, or all your efforts will be wasted.

3. Pour the warm water or milk into the mixing bowl. Use the thermometer to check the temperature of the liquid: It should register at 100°F to 110°F. If your liquids are much hotter than that, you will kill the yeast, which is a living organism. Think of the yeast as a baby: The liquid should be no warmer than a baby's bath. Remember that if your bowl is cold the liquid will become cooler, so measure the temperature of the liquid in the bowl and not before.

4. Sprinkle the yeast on top of the water and let it dissolve. The yeast will float on the surface of the liquid and then sink to the bottom. You can speed the process by stirring, but it will only take about five minutes to dissolve, so why rush things? Take the time to enjoy the process and to appreciate the aroma of the yeast.

5. Add the other ingredients as directed by the recipe. Mix thoroughly so that sugar and salt will dissolve completely into the mixture. Remember that in some bread recipes enriching ingredients like butter or fruits may be added later—follow the instructions carefully. A soft fruit like prunes or even raisins can turn to mush if added too soon.

6. Add the flour gradually, a cup or two at a time, and stir until the flour is fully incorporated into a smooth batter each time. Thorough mixing at this stage also helps incorporate more air into the dough.

7. Once you've added enough flour into the mixture that the dough begins to pull away from the sides of the bowl and is difficult to stir, it's time to abandon the spoon and get your hands in the dough, or more accurately, one hand. Hold the edge of the bowl with one hand, and with the other, mix the dough by pulling up one side, folding it over the top of the rest of the dough, and pressing firmly with your fist. This is the sticky, messy part, but don't be discouraged! Keep mixing with your hand until all the flour and bits of dough are incorporated into a single mass. Remember that you will not be adding all the flour at this stage—some of it is reserved for the kneading stage.

8. Sprinkle about a tablespoon of flour out onto a clean, dry countertop and set the dough on top. Try to get as much of the dough off your fingers as possible, then wash both your hands and the bowl. You'll need a clean, dry bowl to put the dough into later, and the dough will benefit from a short rest at this point as the flour absorbs liquid.

Then both you and the dough will be ready for that most iconic of baking activities: kneading.

Lesson 8:
The Need to Knead

Kneading is the part of bread making that stymies most people: Potential Breadheads aren't sure what to do except mash the dough around aimlessly with disappointing results, the dough is too sticky or becomes too stiff to knead, etc. To develop the skill of kneading, it helps to understand why bakers do it. And that brings us to the subject of gluten.

Before we go any further, let me emphasize that gluten is not a poison or a horrible food additive like trans-fats or MSG. Products are labeled "gluten free" for the sake of people who are allergic to that particular protein or have trouble digesting it, in the same way that dairy products are fine for most people but cause problems for the lactose intolerant. Gluten-free baking is a specialized field, and we won't address it here, but it's certainly a sign of progress that gluten-free products are beginning to be available for the sake of those who need them. Okay, back to our mass of dough on the countertop.

The wheat flour in our dough contains several different proteins, but among them are glutenin and gliadin. Glutenin gives bread dough its elasticity; gliadin makes it soft. When these two protein molecules combine with the water in a recipe, they form a more complex molecule called gluten. Gluten is stretchy and easily forms bonds with itself, and during the process of kneading the gluten is formed into long strands of protein that fold back on themselves and create a kind of net, what I sometimes call "the gluten matrix."

This net of protein captures the CO_2 produced by the yeast as it consumes the sugars in the dough, which makes the dough rise. Without developing this gluten matrix, the gases produced by fermentation will simply dissipate through the surface of the dough. The gluten matrix gives the dough an interior structure, so that it will hold its shape even when it is baked "free-form" without a pan.

As we saw in the section on flours, different kinds of flour have varying amounts of protein: Bread flour has plenty, cake flour hardly any. Grains like rye, corn, and barley are also low in gluten and are usually combined with wheat flour in a bread recipe. The amount of protein in wheat flour is also variable depending upon the kind of wheat used, soil conditions, etc. Since protein is what absorbs the liquid in dough, these variations are the reason why bread recipes do not give an exact amount of flour but a range, e.g., 5½ to 6 cups of flour.

For a fuller explanation of this subject, you can do no better than to read Shirley O. Corriher's outstanding volume Cookwise (William Morrow, 1997). This fascinating book, subtitled The Hows & Whys of Successful Cooking, explains the matter with charts and illustrations in great detail. But bread is just the beginning. You'll also find out why cakes fail, how to make fluffy scrambled eggs, what makes smooth gravy possible, and what brining does for a roast chicken. A James Beard Cookbook Award winner.

So now that you have some idea of what kneading does, let's get down to the business of how to do it. The following instructions and illustrations/photos will help demystify the process of kneading. A note to the Internet savvy: Go online and search for videos on "How to knead bread dough." There will be slight variations in the way each person kneads, but watching the process a few times before attempting it will be helpful.

1. Lightly dust your hands and the countertop with flour.

2. Place the dough close to you on the countertop and lightly grasp the top edge of the dough. Pull the dough back on itself, folding it towards you.

3. With your fingertips on the edge closest to you, press down gently and roll the dough away from you, pushing lightly on the dough as it rolls under your hands. Your fingers should roll off the dough so that you end up with the heels of your palms pushing on the front edge.

Okay, assuming you're trying this for the first time and you have one eye on the dough and one eye on this book, you may have already run into problems on your first try—do not despair! Most likely the dough is sticking to your hands or to the counter or both. You may not have enough flour on your hands or the countertop, but it's more likely that you are either pushing too hard or working too slowly. Press down *gently* on the dough as you roll it forward, and don't be quite as tentative as you work. You want to work with the dough, not against it. Dust a little more flour on your hands and try again:

4. Give the dough a quarter turn, so that one side is now positioned at the top. Pull the top edge back over the dough again, press down gently with your fingertips on the edge closest to you and roll the dough forward with a little more confidence. Better?

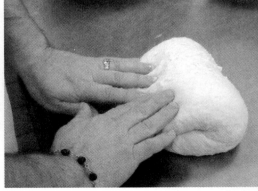

5. Give the dough another quarter turn and keep repeating the process. Try to establish a comfortable and consistent rhythm: fold, push, and turn; fold, push, and turn. Add small amounts of flour to the countertop as you work to keep the dough manageable—no more than a couple of teaspoons at a time. Too much flour results in a dry, crumbly loaf, so it's better to err on the side of a slight stickiness.

Like any other physical activity, kneading requires some practice in order to master it. Find one of your friends or relatives who bakes regularly and ask for a lesson or two. They'll be happy to share their expertise, because they know firsthand just how satisfying it is to learn to knead properly.

How long should you knead? Most recipes call for 6 to 8 minutes of kneading, although some multigrain breads require up to 12 minutes. Set a timer, or find two songs that add up to 8 minutes and knead to the beat. The goal is to produce a dough that is smooth and elastic. "Smooth" in this case does not mean perfectly smooth like glass, but more like the surface of an orange, and you should not feel any lumps or inconsistencies within the dough—unless you've added nuts or raisins! "Elastic" means that when you push down on the dough, it tries to spring back to its original shape. That's the sign that you've developed the gluten matrix that forms the structure of the dough and allows it to rise.

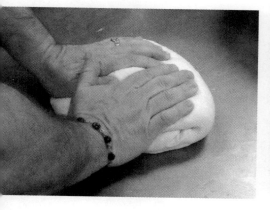
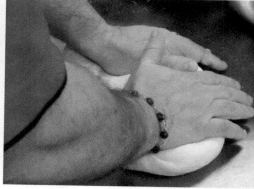

Spring Break

So now that you have a lively, elastic dough on the counter before you, it's time for it to take a nap. Put the dough back into your clean mixing bowl, lightly oil the surface of the dough to keep it from drying out (cooking spray does the job nicely), and lay a clean, dry dish towel on top. The dough is going to rise for the next hour or so during the process of fermentation.

But where to put the bowl? Traditional recipes instruct you to put it in a "warm place free from drafts," a holdover from frontier days when there was no such thing as central heating or foam insulation. The test kitchens of commercial yeast companies recommend 80°F for optimum rising, but the temperature of the average modern kitchen will do just fine. In fact, when bread dough rises more slowly in a slightly cooler place—say 65°F or even lower—the resulting loaves will have a more complex flavor and better texture, although the bread will take longer to rise.

The champion of the slow-rise method is Peter Reinhart, and his book <u>Brother Juniper's Bakery: Slow-rise as Method and Metaphor</u> (Running Press, 2005) is the finest book on the subject, equal parts cookbook, memoir, and meditation. His reflections will make you think differently about the whole process of baking bread. His recipes take more time, but the slow-rise method really does produce a loaf with superior flavor.

Lesson 9:
Punching Down, Shaping, and Baking

Many people ask me how to tell when dough is sufficiently risen to move on to the shaping stage. Visually, it's when the dough has doubled in volume. For a two-loaf batch in a five-quart bowl, that means that the dough has risen almost to the rim of the bowl (see photo on page 52). Another time-honored test is to poke a finger in the middle of the dough and pull it out: If the hole remains and the dough deflates slightly, it's ready.

Next you "punch the dough down"; that is, you push your closed fist into the center of the dough. There is no need to actually *punch* down hard, just use your fist to deflate the dough. Turn the dough out onto the counter and knead it briefly to expel the larger gas bubbles and incorporate a little more oxygen. Cover the dough with a dish towel and let it rest for about 10 minutes. That will allow the gluten strands to relax a bit, which makes the dough easier to shape.

Shaping
Directions for several ways to shape the dough into different kinds of breads are on the pages following each of the basic recipes in this book. Follow the individual recipes, which will provide you with detailed instructions.

Baking
Each oven has its own peculiarities, so it may take several baking trials before you get used to how yours works. Some ovens are hotter at the back of the baking chamber than the front or may be cooler near the bottom. If you have uneven heat in your oven, rotate the bread pans 180 degrees halfway through the baking process. As noted before, your oven's thermostat may not be accurate, especially on older models, so you

may want to invest in a good oven thermometer so you can test yours. Unless the recipe tells you otherwise, always preheat your oven to the recommended temperature before placing the loaves in it for baking.

You'll notice that most recipes give you a range for baking times (e.g., 45 to 55 minutes). The type and size of the oven, the material of the baking pans, the humidity of the kitchen, and many other factors can affect how long it takes for bread to be fully baked. The traditional test for doneness is to thump the bottom of the loaf after removing it from the pan; if it sounds hollow, it's done. Underdone bread often sticks to the pan. If it's been removed too early, it can be placed immediately back in the oven for more baking.

Although I resisted using one for many years, I now rely on an instant-read thermometer to test the temperature of my breads. Fully baked bread has an interior temperature of 195°F to 205°F. White yeast breads and lighter breads like dinner rolls are baked to the lower temperature; I find a slightly higher temperature is better for heavier multi-grain breads. You simply insert the thermometer into the center of the loaf (either the top or the bottom) and read the temperature.

After the bread comes out of the oven it is actually still baking, so resist the temptation (which will be considerable) to cut into the loaf immediately. If you wait 20 minutes or so before slicing, the bread will still be warm but will not be doughy on the inside. Moisture from the center of the loaf works its way outward during the cooling period, which is why you want to cool your breads on a wire rack instead of a flat countertop. Otherwise, the bottom crust will get soggy.

Lesson 10:
How to Choose and Use a Bread Knife

First off, some breads are meant to be torn into hunks rather than sliced: Baguettes and fougasse come to mind, for example. But to a dedicated Breadhead who has labored mightily over a perfectly shaped and baked loaf, there is nothing more disheartening than to see that precious gift squished and torn by a bad bread knife. This is a two-fold problem caused by the condition of the knife and the inexperience of the one wielding it.

Contrary to popular belief, the best blades for slicing bread are not serrated but *wavy*. The points on a serrated knife can tear the bread and cause an abundance of crumbs, and it's even worse if the knife is dull. A wavy knife blade by contrast slices easily even through the crustiest loaf and is more easily sharpened than the serrated kind. They also cut angel food cakes like nobody's business.

Unfortunately, even expensive, professional-grade bread knives are often serrated, so you may have to look around awhile to find a good wavy knife, and it may not be cheap. That being said, I found one of my favorite wavy bread knives in a discount store; it has a whopping 10-inch blade, and it cost less than $10.

Another option is to look in antique malls and on eBay for a vintage bread knife. The best were made by the Klauss Knife Company of Fremont, Ohio, in the first half of the twentieth century, and they came in different lengths with varying degrees of decoration. When I see one in an antique shop or flea market, I buy it immediately, no matter how rusty it looks: A professional knife sharpener can restore it to its former glory and usefulness. I purchased a few on eBay as well, but be sure to compare prices.

Now to the business of slicing technique. It's really quite simple: A gentle sawing motion without much downward pressure is the best method for slicing everything from a crusty baguette to a soft potato bread still warm from the oven. Large round loaves are best sliced in a herringbone pattern (see illustration), and don't let anyone cut *both* crusts of a rectangular loaf: You need to leave one intact to be able to get even slices all the way to the end. The width of the slice is up to you of course, but take into account the width of the slots on your toaster and the size of your waistband!

Lesson 11:
Storing Your Bread

The first principal of storing bread is that it should never be wrapped in plastic unless it is absolutely stone cold, which could take up to three hours after baking. As noted earlier, moisture works its way out of the interior of the loaf as it cools, and that moisture will be trapped in the bag and settle on the bread, resulting in a soggy crust. If you bake at night and don't want to wait up, wrap your loaf loosely in a clean, dry towel, and it will be fine in the morning. Crusty loaves will often go soft when wrapped in plastic, so an open-ended paper bag will do for them.

Bread also keeps well when frozen. If your bread will be used within a week or two, a single layer of plastic wrap or a re-used bread bag will do the trick. But ordinary plastic wrap and bread bags are not completely air-tight: When I put 10 loaves of herb bread in the car to deliver to a parish bake sale, I can smell them the whole way there! For longer storage (up to about three months) wrap your loaves once in plastic and again in carefully sealed aluminum foil, or place the wrapped loaf in a freezer-safe bag.

Homework:

Okay class, before we begin the practicum section of this Breadhead Course, here's a little homework assignment. Try this bread recipe that requires only two ingredients: self-rising flour and melted ice cream.

Ice Cream Muffins

Yields 6 muffins.

1 cup self-rising flour (see note)
1½ cups melted ice cream, any flavor

Preheat oven to 375°F. Place flour into a medium bowl. Stir in melted ice cream to make a thick batter. If the ice cream has chocolate chips or nuts, make sure they get mixed in, too. You can also add nuts, candy, or fruit to the mix.

Lightly grease a six-cup muffin tin. Divide batter among muffin cups. Bake for 10 to 12 minutes, or until a toothpick inserted into the center of a muffin comes out clean. The tops of the muffins may not brown very much, but the tops should spring back when lightly pressed.

Let muffins cool to lukewarm, then eat immediately. Feel free to dunk pieces of the muffin in the remaining melted ice cream.

NOTES

— Self-rising flour is simply all-purpose flour with baking soda and salt added. If you don't have self-rising flour in hand, you can substitute 1 cup of all-purpose flour, 1½ teaspoons of baking powder, and ½ teaspoon of salt.

— IMPORTANT: Self-rising flour is used for quick breads like muffins and biscuits. It is NOT used for any of the other recipes for yeast breads in this book. So if you buy a five-pound bag of self-rising flour, you'll have to make this recipe 17 times to use it all up. Darn.

A muffin thief!

Basic White Dough

The foundation for literally hundreds of recipes, mastering Basic White Dough will give you a starting point for your journey of exploration of the world of breads. After you get this down, it's all about the shaping.

2 cups warm water (100°F to 110°F)
2 pkg. active dry yeast
2 Tbs. granulated sugar
2 tsp. salt
2 Tbs. vegetable oil
5½ to 6 cups all-purpose or bread flour

Dissolve yeast in warm water in a large mixing bowl. Add sugar, oil, and salt, and mix well. Add 5 cups of flour, one cup at a time, mixing well after each cup. Knead for 5 to 8 minutes, adding more flour as needed to make a smooth and elastic dough that is only slightly sticky. Lightly oil the surface of the dough and place in a clean, dry bowl. Cover with a dry cloth and let rise about an hour or until doubled. Punch the dough down, and knead it lightly. Shape the loaves as directed according to the individual instructions that follow.

NOTES

— There are lots of variations on this Basic White Dough regarding the amount of water, sugar, salt, and oil. I like this one because everything is in "twos" except the flour, so it's easy to carry in your head.

— Remember that bread flour has more protein than all-purpose (see page 15) so it will absorb more liquid. You may use less of it if you are used to making bread with all-purpose flour.

— Don't move on to wheat or sweet dough until you become proficient in the skills needed for this recipe. Later on, you'll be glad you took the time to practice.

free form
standard loaf pan
pull apart garlic bread
chewy dinner rolls
pizza
pretzels

Free Form Loaves

These are the classic round or oval breads you see in country markets. Yields two loaves.

1 batch of Basic White Dough, risen once (page 36)

Punch down dough and knead briefly to expel larger air bubbles. Divide dough into two equal portions. Lightly dust your hands with flour. Grasp the portion of dough on opposite sides and pull gently to stretch the top. Tuck the ends under and pinch them gently. Give the dough a quarter turn and repeat, again stretching the top into a smooth surface; tuck the ends under and pinch. Repeat as necessary to form a smooth round of dough with some tension on the top. This tight surface will hold the gases better and make for a higher, lighter loaf. Repeat with the other portion of dough. You may also roll the dough gently on the countertop under your palm to form an oval shape.

Place the loaves on a lightly greased baking sheet, evenly spaced. Cover with a clean, dry cloth and let rise for 30 minutes or until almost doubled. Bake in a preheated 375°F oven on the middle rack for 20 to 25 minutes, or until loaves are lightly browned and sound hollow when tapped. The interior temperature of the loaf should be about 195°F. Cool on a wire rack.

NOTES

— To make a more decorative top to these loaves, you can slash the tops with a sharp knife or razor blade just before they go into the oven. Be warned, however: If the dough has risen for too long, this slashing will cause them to deflate, and they may turn out low and rather dense. You can avoid this by slashing them about two-thirds of the way through the final rising. And if you doubt the sharpness of your slashing tool, don't even attempt it!

— You can also form long baguettes by rolling the dough gently under both palms using an even, steady pressure as you roll. These loaves look especially nice when slashed diagonally about five times down the length of the loaf.

Authentic French baguettes require a considerably more involved process, including several risings. Bernard Clayton's _New Complete Book of Breads_ (Simon & Schuster, 1987) contains detailed, step-by-step instructions. It has hundreds of bread recipes and even in paperback it's a relatively expensive book, so check it out from the library first or wait until you get a gift card. I received my copy from a dear friend who found it at a garage sale. Her inscription: "I'll take a half dozen each!"

Standard Loaf Pan

Your baloney sandwiches will be a whole order of magnitude better with this bread. Remember to use the medium-size pans (8½ × 4½ × 2½ inches) for this amount of dough. Yields two loaves.

1 batch of Basic White Dough, risen once (page 36)

Punch down dough and knead briefly to expel larger air bubbles. Divide dough into two equal portions. Lightly dust your hands with flour. Grasp the portion of dough on opposite sides and pull gently to stretch the top. Tuck the ends under and pinch them gently. Give the dough a quarter turn and repeat, again stretching the top into a smooth surface; tuck the ends under and pinch. Repeat as necessary to form a smooth round of dough with some tension on the top. This tight surface will hold the gases better and make for a higher, lighter loaf. Roll the dough gently on the countertop under your palm to form an oval shape about 8 inches long. Place the dough in a lightly greased loaf pan with the smoothest side facing upwards. Repeat with the other portion of dough.

Cover with a clean, dry cloth and let rise for 30 minutes or until almost doubled. Bake in a preheated 375°F oven on the middle rack for 35 to 40 minutes, or until loaves are lightly browned and sound hollow when tapped. Remember to rotate the pans 180 degrees halfway through the baking process. The interior temperature of the loaf should be about 195°F. Cool on a wire rack.

NOTES

— The surface of the pan you use will affect the color of the crust on the sides and bottom. A bright, shiny pan will produce a lighter crust (even when fully baked), whereas a pan with a darker surface will produce a correspondingly darker crust.

— If you prefer a softer top crust, you can wait until the loaves are out of the oven about 10 minutes and then brush the tops with a little melted butter. This step produces a richer color to the loaf as well.

Ernie, a Breadhead student, took this recipe in a different direction to bake six mini-loaves.

Pull Apart Garlic Bread

This bread pulls apart in sections with herbed garlic butter on all sides. Yields two loaves.

1 batch of Basic White Dough, risen once (page 36)

Herbed Garlic Butter

½ cup melted butter (NOT margarine or diet spread)
2 Tbs. dried parsley
1 Tbs. dried Italian seasoning mix
1 Tbs. granulated garlic (more if stronger garlic flavor is desired)
2 Tbs. beaten egg

Mix all ingredients for garlic butter in a bowl. Divide the batch of Basic White Dough into two portions. Divide a portion into 12 pieces. Lightly dust your hands with flour and roll each piece of dough on the countertop to form a smooth ball. Dip each piece into the butter mixture, coating completely. Arrange in a single layer—you'll have to squish them a little—in a 9 × 5 inch greased loaf pan. Repeat with the second portion of dough in its own pan. Let rise until the dough just reaches the top of the pan, then bake in a preheated 375°F oven for about 35 to 40 minutes. About 10 minutes before the bread is done, you can brush the tops with some of the remaining beaten egg and sprinkle with Parmesan cheese. Remove from pans and serve warm.

This Pull Apart Garlic Bread was baked in a mini-loaf pan, a good presentation option if you have number of smaller tables to serve.

NOTES

— If you have fresh herbs, by all means use them, but double the amounts.

— If you don't have the large 9 × 5 inch pans, use medium-size pans. Sometimes the butter mixture will spill out of the pans, so I set them on a cookie sheet to catch any drips. Otherwise, you have to clean the bottom of the oven, and in an electric oven there can be a danger of fire (this is a matter of personal experience!).

— You can serve this bread on a buffet with a platter of cheese and Italian beef on the side. Break open a roll, tuck in a generous portion of beef and a slice of provolone, and you have a party sandwich second to none. Great for picnics, too.

Chewy Dinner Rolls

For these delights you'll need one more piece of equipment: a water sprayer, like the kind you use to mist plants. Do NOT re-use a spray bottle that once held window cleaner or some other chemical. You'll also need a baking sheet. Yields one dozen small rolls.

½ batch of Basic White Dough, risen once (page 36). It wouldn't hurt to knead the dough an extra minute or two, and be sure to use bread flour rather than all-purpose.

Punch down dough and knead briefly to expel larger air bubbles. Divide dough into twelve small portions. Lightly dust your hands with flour and roll a portion of dough on the countertop to form a smooth ball. Repeat with the other portions of dough.

Place the rolls on two lightly greased baking sheets, evenly spaced (rows of 2, 3, 2, 3, and 2 rolls). Cover with a clean, dry cloth and let rise for about 30 minutes or until almost doubled. Preheat the oven to 400°F. About five minutes before baking time, spray water on the sides of the oven about ten times (five per side), being careful not to spray water on the oven light, fan, or heating elements. Spray again at baking time, and place the rolls in the preheated oven. Repeat the spraying procedure after two minutes, and again two minutes after that, each time closing the door quickly so the oven doesn't lose too much heat. Bake for another 10 to 12 minutes, or until rolls are lightly browned. The interior temperature of the rolls should be about 195°F. (You only need to check one of them.) Remove from pan and cool on a wire rack.

NOTES

— The introduction of steam into the oven does two things. First, it keeps the tops of the rolls from drying out too quickly, so you get a fuller rise and lighter rolls (it works with full bread loaves, too). The moisture on the surface of the dough also causes a chewy crust to form. Some bakers maintain that spraying the oven produces better steam than the pan method, described below. Try both, and you decide!

— Another way to introduce steam into the oven is to place ½ cup of hot water in a shallow pan on the bottom shelf of the oven 10 minutes before baking and omit the spraying.

— These rolls are best eaten the day they are baked or shortly thereafter.

— You may make larger rolls by dividing the dough into eight portions.

Pizza

Basic white bread dough makes a pretty good homemade pizza crust, too. Makes three 12-inch medium-thick crusts.

1 batch of Basic White Dough, risen once (page 36)

Preheat oven to 450°F. Punch down dough and knead briefly to expel larger air bubbles. Divide dough into three equal portions. Lightly dust your hands with flour. Grasp the portion of dough on opposite sides and pull gently to stretch the top. Tuck the ends under and pinch them gently. Give the dough a quarter turn and repeat, again stretching the top into a smooth surface; tuck the ends under and pinch. Repeat as necessary to form a smooth round of dough with some tension on the top. This tight surface will hold the gases better and make for a higher, lighter pizza crust. Repeat with the other portions of dough. Let the portions of dough rest on a lightly greased surface, covered with a clean, dry towel or oiled plastic wrap. Let the balls of dough rest for 10 minutes so the dough can relax before shaping. Believe me, this resting period will make the dough MUCH easier to roll out. Work with one piece of dough at a time, keeping the remaining crusts covered.

To form the crust, place the dough on a lightly floured surface and flatten the dough with your hand. Dust the top lightly with flour to prevent sticking. Roll out with a rolling pin to the desired size, rotating the dough after two or three passes of the rolling pin to ensure a uniform thickness.

Form a slightly raised edge for the crust. You can do this one of two ways: 1) simply push the edge of the dough together with your fingers to form a raised edge; or 2) brush the outer edge of the dough with a little water, then fold the outer edge over and press it down onto the crust. This latter method makes a thicker outer crust, preferable when you are making a pizza with a lot of toppings or if the outer crust is your favorite part.

To ensure a consistent interior texture, some pizzerias "dock" their dough, that is, they pierce it all over with a fork or a specially designed tool called a "docker." This step isn't necessary if you don't mind a few air pockets in the crust. A little tip: When I dock a crust, I use the points on a plastic pasta server.

Place the crust on a lightly oiled pizza pan and add desired toppings. Bake for 15 to 25 minutes, depending on how crisp you want the crust and how dark you want the cheese on top. If the cheese gets too dark on your first try, bake the second pizza without cheese for 5 or 10 minutes and remove it from the oven. Add the cheese and return the pizza to the oven to finish baking.

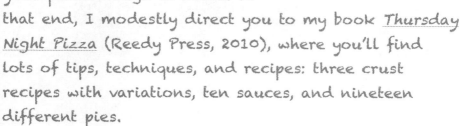

There are a lot of ways—some simple, some more complex—to improve the quality of your pizza dough at home. To that end, I modestly direct you to my book _Thursday Night Pizza_ (Reedy Press, 2010), where you'll find lots of tips, techniques, and recipes: three crust recipes with variations, ten sauces, and nineteen different pies.

Father Ronald's heirloom tomatoes on a four cheese pizza with Italian herbs

NOTES

— If you don't have a round pizza pan, you can roll this dough out into a rectangle and cook it on a baking sheet, too. To make truly first-rate pizza at home, you need a pizza stone and a wooden paddle to transfer the pizza onto the hot stone. These instructions are just to get you hooked on the idea of homemade pizza—does that sound too much like a "gateway drug"?—so you'll do some more exploring.

— I suspect you'll find that a light hand with the toppings, especially the sauce and the cheese, will yield better results. If you let a teenager put on the toppings, don't say I didn't warn you.

Pretzels

Try these at home and you may never eat another stadium pretzel again. A large, deep skillet works just fine for boiling the pretzels before baking, which is what gives them their chewy texture and deep color.

½ batch of **Basic White Dough, risen once (page 36)**
2 quarts water
¼ **cup baking soda**
Coarse salt

Punch dough down, knead lightly to work out the larger air bubbles, then allow dough to rest for 10 minutes. Divide dough into eight pieces. Roll each piece out into a rope about 18 inches long. Shape ropes into pretzels. Place pretzels on a lightly greased baking sheet and allow to rise for 15 minutes.

Pour the two quarts of water into a large skillet or pan and bring to a boil. Dissolve the baking soda in the water. Gently lower two or three pretzels into the water at a time and allow them to boil one minute; turn pretzels over and boil for another minute. Gently remove pretzels from water with a pair of tongs or slotted spoon and place on cloth towels to drain. Repeat until all pretzels have been boiled.

Place pretzels on a well-greased baking sheet about ½ inch apart. Sprinkle with coarse salt, then bake at 375°F for 20 to 25 minutes. Cool slightly on wire racks and serve warm.

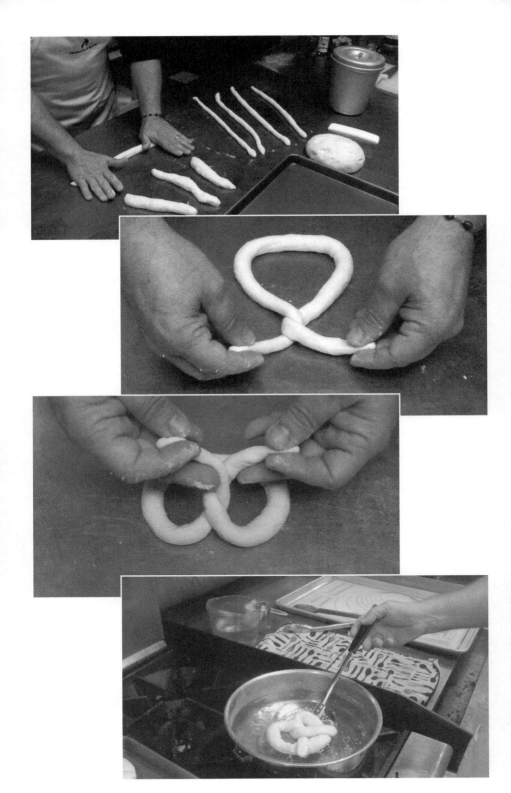

NOTES

— You may of course use a whole batch of Basic White Dough and make sixteen pretzels or take the second portion and bake a free form loaf in the same oven.

— If you find that the pretzels stick to your baking sheets after baking, you might want to invest in a non-stick silicon mat.

— Many pretzel recipes call for barley malt syrup instead of sugar. It can be found in most health food stores, but you can also substitute brown sugar, molasses, or a strong honey for the granulated sugar in the Basic White Dough recipe.

— Roll the portions of dough into a shorter length (about 12 inches) and you can make pretzel rolls that will serve as a hamburger bun or sandwich roll—yum!

Use half the batch of dough for your pretzels and the other half for a loaf of bread. An afternoon snack plus homemade bread for supper—what could be better?

Basic Wheat Dough

This recipe yields a fairly light wheat dough that is rather hearty.

2¼ cups warm water (100°F to 110°F)
2 pkg. active dry yeast
2 Tbs. brown sugar
2 tsp. salt
2 Tbs. vegetable oil
2 cups whole wheat flour
3½ to 4 cups bread flour

Mixed dough

Risen dough

NOTES

— Because whole wheat flour has proportionally less protein by volume than white flour, bread flour is recommended for this recipe to increase the amount of gluten in the dough. Otherwise, the resulting loaf may be rather dense and heavy.

Punch down

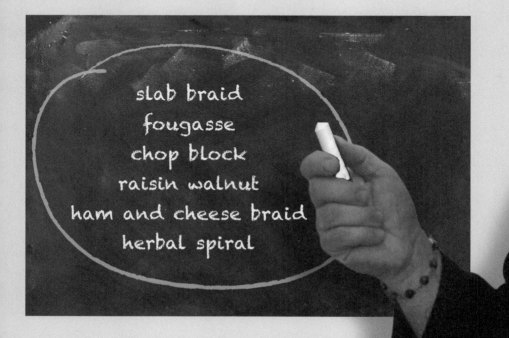

Slab Braid

A beautiful braided loaf is easy to create with this simple method—far easier than trying to roll out perfectly even ropes of dough.

½ batch of Basic Wheat Dough, risen once (page 52)

Punch down dough and knead briefly to expel larger air bubbles. Allow dough to rest for 10 minutes so the gluten strands will relax and it will be easier to roll out. Lightly dust the countertop with flour. Using a lightly dusted rolling pin, roll dough into a thick oval about 12 × 6 inches (you may need to sprinkle a small amount of flour on the dough as you work). Take a pizza cutter or pastry wheel and make two long parallel cuts in the oval, dividing the slab evenly into three sections. BUT do not cut all the way through at the top—leave the three strips connected at the top—see illustrations. Braid the three strips and tuck the ends under at the bottom.

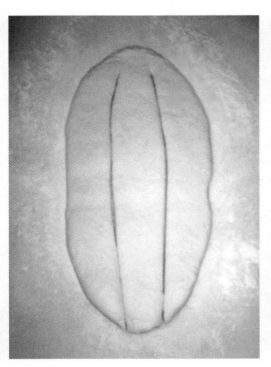 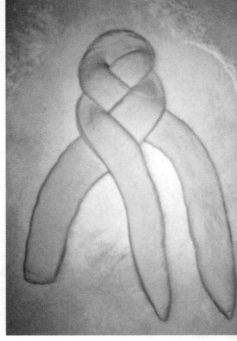

Carefully place the braid on a lightly greased baking sheet. Cover with a clean, dry cloth and let rise for 30 minutes or until almost doubled. Bake in a preheated 375°F oven on the middle rack for 20 to 25 minutes, or until loaf is lightly browned and sounds hollow when tapped. The interior temperature of the loaf should be about 200°F. Remove from pan and cool on a wire rack.

NOTES

— You can make a slab braid using any bread dough in this recipe book or other recipes.

— You can make this loaf even more beautiful by brushing the top with a little milk and sprinkling on poppy seeds just before the loaf goes in the oven.

If you want to see what various kinds of washes and toppings can do to the surface of a loaf of bread, look at _Ultimate Bread_ (DK, 1998), by Eric Treuille and Ursula Ferrigno, which includes photos of bread brushed with milk, egg wash, honey, and other liquids, each of which creates a different effect. There are more than 100 inspiring recipes drawn from bread-making traditions around the world, and the beautiful photos will inspire you to tie on an apron and fire up the oven. One of my all-time favorite bread books.

Fougasse

This classic bread can be made with just about any dough and can be sweet with dried fruit or savory with herbs and onions. Once you master the shaping technique, feel free to experiment.

1 batch of Basic Wheat Dough, risen once (page 52)

Punch the dough down and knead it lightly to work out the larger air pockets; divide dough into two portions. Cover with a clean, dry cloth and let rest 10 minutes to allow the gluten strands to relax so it will be easier to roll out.

On a lightly floured surface, roll each piece out into an oval about ½ inch thick. Place each piece on its own lightly greased baking sheet. Using a pastry wheel or small pizza cutter, make five or six slashes in dough as illustrated. Pull the slashes apart slightly to enlarge the openings so they don't close up during rising and baking. Repeat with the second portion of dough and place on its own baking sheet. Cover with a dry cloth and let rise for 30 to 45 minutes. Bake at 400°F for 20 to 25 minutes, until bread sounds hollow when tapped. Cool on racks.

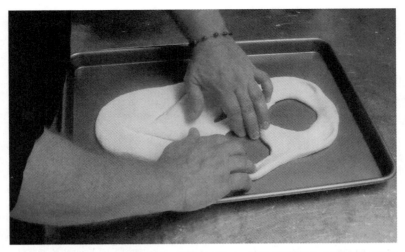

NOTES

— The French word *fougasse* is related to the Italian *focaccia*. Both come from the Latin word *focus*, meaning "hearth." Both breads were cooked on a flat stone placed on the embers of the fire.

— If you have a pizza stone, you might consider making smaller loaves that fit on the stone. Be sure to put the stone in the oven as it heats up, and allow for extra time for the stone to reach the proper temperature.

— Olives are a traditional addition to fougasse, so add a cup of coarsely chopped olives to the dough at the kneading stage if you like their flavor.

Breads cooked on a flat stone or griddle are found all over the world. _Flatbreads and Flavors_ (William Morrow, 2008), by Jeffry Alford and Naomi Duguid, will take you on a fascinating tour of countries, cultures, and kitchens with detailed recipes from tortillas to pita to naan to chapatti. Part travelogue and part cookbook, this James Beard Award winner is a cookbook every Breadhead needs within easy reach.

Chop Block Bread

Like many others, this bread can be made with just about any kind of dough as long as it's not too sweet, but it really is best with wheat dough.

1 batch of Basic Wheat Dough, risen once (page 52)
¼ cup chopped celery
2 cups finely chopped onion
2 cups chopped carrots
2 cups coarsely chopped broccoli
1 cup grated sharp cheddar

Toss all vegetables with the cheese in a bowl until evenly blended. Punch down dough and knead briefly to work out large air bubbles. Pat dough out into a large oval. Place vegetables on top and fold the dough in half. Knead gently to distribute the vegetables. At first, the dough will fall apart and be a bit awkward to handle, but be patient and keep pushing rogue veggies back into the dough. Eventually, the vegetables become incorporated, but without losing their shape.

Grease a large baking sheet. Flatten the dough into a large oval about 1½ inches thick and place on the baking sheet. Cover and let rise in a warm place free from drafts for 30 to 45 minutes, until nearly doubled in bulk. Bake in a preheated oven at 350°F for 40 to 50 minutes. Cover loaf lightly with aluminum foil if it begins to brown too quickly. The loaf is done when top crust is firm and sounds hollow when tapped (195°F to 200°F in the interior). Cool on a rack.

NOTES

— The cheese in the bread can make it brown quickly, so keep an eye on these loaves in the first 20 or 30 minutes to make sure they aren't turning too dark. You can also try other kinds of cheese—I recommend Romano, for example—or perhaps substituting cauliflower or olives for one of the other ingredients. A couple of teaspoons of dried sage and thyme wouldn't hurt either.

This is meant to be a rustic loaf, so leave the bread knife in the drawer and just tear off a hunk to dunk in your soup.

Raisin Walnut Bread

This bread makes good toast, but it's also a great base for chicken salad sandwiches. Yields two loaves.

1 batch of Basic Wheat Dough, risen once (see page 52)
2 cups dark raisins
1 cup walnuts, medium chopped

Punch down dough and knead briefly to work out the larger air bubbles. Roll the dough out to a thickness of about ½ inch. Sprinkle nuts and raisins on top of the dough. Fold the edges of the dough toward the center and knead for a few minutes to distribute the raisins and nuts evenly. At first it will be messy and seem to be falling apart, but be patient; it will all come together.

Let dough rest for about 10 minutes, then divide dough into two equal portions. Lightly dust your hands with flour. Grasp the portion of dough on opposite sides and pull gently to stretch the top. Tuck the ends under and pinch them gently. Give the dough a quarter turn and repeat, again stretching the top into a smooth surface; tuck the ends under and pinch. Repeat as necessary to form a round of dough with some tension on the top. This tight surface will hold the gases better and make for a higher, lighter loaf.

Roll the dough gently on the countertop under your palm to form an oval shape about 8 inches long. Repeat with the other portion of dough. Place loaves in lightly greased medium loaf pans (8½ × 4½ × 2½ inches) and cover with a clean, dry towel. Let rise for 40 minutes or until nearly doubled in bulk. Preheat the oven to 350°F. Bake for 35 to 45 minutes, or until loaves are golden brown and sound hollow when tapped. Remove from pans and cool on racks.

— You will love the flavor and the texture of this bread: sweet, nutty, earthy, and wholesome. You can use other nuts, like pecans, or try toasted sunflower seeds.

— When you shop for raisins for this recipe, don't buy "baking raisins" because they are softer and really meant for cookies and muffins—in the kneaded dough they turn to mush.

Ham and Cheese Lattice Braid

This is a fairly simple technique but it yields dramatic results, and the loaf looks especially nice on a holiday buffet table. Yields one loaf.

½ batch of Basic Wheat Dough, risen once (page 52)
1½ cups coarsely chopped ham
1½ cups sharp cheddar cheese
1 egg beaten with 1 Tbs. of water for egg wash (optional)

Punch down dough and knead lightly to expel larger air bubbles. Cover with a clean, dry cloth and let rest 10 minutes to allow the gluten strands to relax so it will be easier to roll out. On a lightly floured board, roll out to a rectangle about 18 × 10 inches. Prepare filling by combining ham and cheese in a medium-size bowl and tossing to mix. Spread filling lengthwise in the center third of the dough, pressing it together lightly.

Using a sharp knife or a small pizza cutter, cut each outer third of the dough (the part not covered by the filling) into 5 to 10 diagonal strips, cutting from the edge of the dough to about 1 inch from the edge of the filling (see photos). Lightly brush strips with water. Fold strips over filling, alternating left and right, being careful not to stretch the dough. Tuck in the ends of the last strips and pinch to seal. Carefully transfer to a lightly greased baking pan. Cover and let rise in a warm, draft-free place for 30 minutes or until doubled in size.

If desired, brush surface of loaf with egg wash. Bake in a preheated 375°F oven on the middle shelf for 30 minutes or until golden brown and the temperature of the filling is at least 160°F. Allow the loaf to cool on the pan for 10 minutes before removing to a wire rack to cool slightly before serving.

NOTES

— I have taught this technique to every level of baker, including junior high and high school students, and the results have always been spectacular. Just make sure you don't roll the dough out too wide (use a ruler to check the dimensions) and you should do just fine.

— For a more interesting texture, add a half cup of chopped walnuts to the filling.

— Different fillers can be used with this recipe. For instance, the images here show an apple filling, which is much more photogenic than ham and cheese.

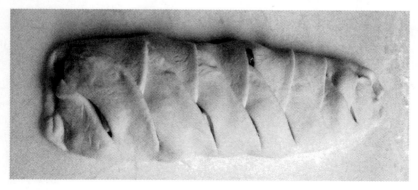

Herbal Spiral

One Sunday I went out to my garden and came back in with several Mason jars filled with fragrant herbs. I knew that we were getting a pasta dish for supper that night, so I created this recipe on the spot. Feel free to adjust the kinds of herbs. Yields two loaves.

1 batch of Basic Wheat Dough, risen once (see page 52)
1 cup ricotta cheese
½ cup fresh parsley leaves
1 cup snipped chives
¼ cup fresh oregano leaves
½ cup fresh basil leaves
Salt and pepper

NOTE: All herbs should be loosely packed when measured.

Coarsely chop parsley, oregano, and basil leaves and toss together with the chives until mixed. Punch down dough and knead lightly to expel larger air bubbles; divide dough into two portions. Cover with a clean, dry cloth and let rest 10 minutes to allow the gluten strands to relax so it will be easier to roll out. On a lightly floured countertop, roll one portion into a rectangle 12 inches wide and 14 inches long. Spread ½ cup of ricotta evenly over the dough and sprinkle on chopped herbs. Sprinkle lightly with salt and pepper. Roll up jelly-roll style and place seam side down on a lightly oiled baking sheet (bend the roll into a curve to fit on the pan if necessary).

Repeat with the second portion of dough and place on a separate pan. Cover loaves with a dry towel and let rise until nearly doubled, about 30 minutes. Make 5 diagonal slashes with a sharp knife or razor blade on the top of each loaf. Bake at 400°F for 15 to 20 minutes. Bread is done when it is lightly browned and sounds hollow when tapped; the interior temperature should be between 195°F and 200°F. Leave the loaves on the pan for about 10 minutes before transferring to wire racks using a pair of large metal spatulas.

NOTES

— A little advice about rolling out dough: Giving the dough a rest as directed will allow the gluten strands to relax after kneading, so that it rolls out more easily. After the rest, pat the dough into a thick rectangle before dusting it lightly with flour and rolling it out with a rolling pin. Keep the surface of the dough lightly dusted with flour to prevent it from sticking to the rolling pin, and sprinkle a teaspoon or two on the countertop as needed throughout the process.

— You can use the Basic White Dough recipe for this bread as well (see page 36).

Basic Sweet Dough

2 cups milk
¼ cup butter
5¾ to 6¼ cups all-purpose flour
1 beaten egg
¼ cup sugar
1½ tsp. salt
2 pkg. yeast, proofed in ¼ cup warm water

Proof the yeast by mixing it in a small bowl with ¼ cup of warm water (about 100°F; see notes). Heat milk in a saucepan, but do not boil. Add butter, sugar, and salt; mix well and cool to lukewarm. Pour into mixing bowl along with proofed yeast and the beaten egg. One cup at a time, add five cups of flour, mixing thoroughly each time until the flour is incorporated. Add another ½ cup of flour and mix with your hands until the dough pulls away from the side of the bowl and forms a single mass.

Remove from bowl and turn out onto a lightly floured surface and knead for five or six minutes, adding more flour as needed to form a smooth, elastic dough. Remember that dough for rolls should be softer than most bread dough. Place in a greased bowl and let rise, covered, in a warm place free of drafts until doubled, about 1 to 1½ hours. Punch down dough and knead briefly to expel the larger air bubbles. Shape as directed.

NOTES

— With the egg, butter, and sugar in this dough, the yeast has some heavy lifting to do, so we give it a head start by "proofing" it. The yeast is mixed with ¼ cup of warm water and a pinch of sugar and allowed to develop for 5 or 10 minutes. Add the yeast to the water a little at a time, stirring constantly. Otherwise the yeast will form clumps that are hard to dissolve. I usually stir with an ordinary dinner fork, and it seems to do the trick nicely.

— There is extra liquid in the dough, so it requires slightly more flour than the two previous basic recipes. But since this recipe is generally used for rolls and other softer breads, be very careful not to add so much that the dough gets stiff or dry. If the dough remains a little sticky even after kneading, that won't hurt in the long run.

Braid Top Loaf

This technique yields a standard loaf with a braided top—it looks especially beautiful on a sandwich buffet for a family get-together.

1 batch of Basic Sweet Dough, risen once (page 68)
2 medium loaf pans (8½ × 4½ × 2½ inches)

Punch down dough and knead briefly to expel larger air bubbles. Divide dough into two portions and allow dough to rest for 10 minutes so the gluten strands will relax. Lightly dust the countertop with flour. Using a lightly dusted rolling pin, roll one portion of dough into a thick oval about 9 × 5 inches (you may need to sprinkle a small amount of flour on the dough as you work). Take a pizza cutter or pastry wheel and make two long parallel cuts in the oval, dividing the slab evenly into three sections. BUT do not cut all the way through at the top—leave the three strips connected at the top—see illustrations on page 54. Braid the three strips and tuck the ends under at the bottom. Carefully place the braid in a medium loaf pan. Repeat with second portion of dough. Cover with a clean, dry cloth and let rise for 30 minutes or until almost doubled. Bake in a preheated 375°F oven on the middle rack for 30 to 35 minutes, or until loaf is lightly browned and sounds hollow when tapped. The interior temperature of the loaf should be about 195°F. Remove from pan and cool on a wire rack.

NOTES

— This method is essentially the same thing as a slab braid but placed in a loaf pan so you get a fancier finished product. It's surprisingly simple and makes an impressive display. Make several for a party and slice the loaves ahead of time, but leave one loaf whole to place as a centerpiece of the display.

— A braid top loaf also makes a lovely gift bread when you want something for a special occasion. I keep my eyes open for inexpensive baskets in which to place these loaves, so I can bake a birthday present at the last minute. If the basket is a little larger, you can tuck in a jar or two of homemade preserves on the side.

— You can use the Basic White (see page 36) or Basic Wheat Dough (see page 52) recipes for this method as well.

Crescent Rolls

A classic shape for dinner rolls, and it's easy to make them all the same size. Yields 16 rolls.

½ batch of Basic Sweet Dough, risen once (see page 68)
2 baking sheets

Punch down dough and knead lightly to expel larger air bubbles; divide dough into two portions. Cover with a clean, dry cloth and let rest 10 minutes to allow the gluten strands to relax so it will be easier to roll out. Roll one portion of dough into a circle roughly 18 inches in diameter. With a small pizza cutter or sharp knife, cut into eight equal wedges.

Starting with the wide end of each triangle, roll up and curve the pointed end to shape into crescents (see illustration). Note that the points are curved towards the narrower side of the top layer of dough and the point of the dough ends up on the bottom of the roll. Place the rolls, evenly spaced, on lightly greased cookie sheets. Cover baking sheet with a clean, dry cloth. Repeat with second portion of dough. Allow to rise until nearly doubled in a warm place, free of drafts—about 30 minutes. Bake at 350°F until lightly browned, about 12 to 15 minutes. Remove rolls from pan to cool slightly on wire racks and serve warm.

NOTES

— My mom made crescent rolls often for our family, although her recipe was enriched with sour cream and consequently took longer to rise. This recipe is better for the beginning Breadhead.

— These rolls will not be as large as a sandwich croissant, and not quite as soft. Real croissants are made by creating multiple layers of dough and butter through repeated rollings and foldings of the dough. God alone knows how prepackaged croissants are made.

— Basic Sweet Dough is ideal for other shapes of rolls as well.

The Good Housekeeping Illustrated Cookbook (Hearst Books, 1980) has outstanding directions and illustrations of how to make all sorts of dinner rolls, as well as a very fine section on quick breads like muffins and banana bread. In addition to the dozens of color photos, you'll love the rest of the book's pictures of kitchen basics like how to clean shellfish, cut up a chicken, and prepare vegetables from artichokes to zucchini. It's no longer in print, but a recent online search yielded over 200 copies available from various used booksellers. It's definitely worth the effort to search for it.

Cinnamon Swirl Bread

Cinnamon Swirl toast with butter and a glass of cold milk—the ultimate bedtime snack!

1 batch of Basic Sweet Dough, risen once (page 68)
2 medium loaf pans (8½ × 4½ × 2½ inches)
2 Tbs. cinnamon
½ cup sugar
Pinch of nutmeg
2 Tbs. melted butter

Combine sugar and spices for filling in a small bowl. Punch down dough and knead lightly to expel larger air bubbles; divide dough into two portions. Cover with a clean, dry cloth and let rest 10 minutes so the gluten strands relax and the dough will be easier to roll out.

On a lightly floured countertop, pat one portion of the dough into a fat rectangle and sprinkle lightly with flour. With a floured rolling pin, roll dough into a rectangle about 14 × 7 inches. Spread with melted butter and sprinkle on half the sugar filling, leaving a ½-inch border of "clean dough" on all edges.

Starting with the shorter edge, roll dough up tightly and seal the edges. Place seam side down in a lightly greased medium loaf pan. Repeat with second portion of dough. Cover with a clean, dry towel and let rise until nearly doubled, about 30 minutes. Bake at 375°F for 35 to 40 minutes— loosely cover the loaves with aluminum foil if the tops begin browning too quickly. The interior temperature should be about 195°F. Remove from pans and cool on a wire rack. If desired, while the loaves are still warm, brush the top of the loaves with more butter and sprinkle with additional cinnamon sugar.

NOTES

— Be careful not to add too much flour, either in mixing or kneading, or the dough will be too stiff to roll out. It's better for the dough to be a bit too soft than too stiff.

— When sealing the edges of the loaf, brush the edge of the dough with a little milk if you have trouble getting it to stick.

— You can of course add a cup or two of raisins to the filling.

Cinnamon Rolls

1 batch of Basic Sweet Dough, risen once (page 68)
2 Tbs. cinnamon
⅓ cup sugar
⅓ cup brown sugar
2 Tbs. butter, melted

Combine sugar and spices for filling in a small bowl. Punch down dough and knead lightly to expel larger air bubbles; divide dough into two portions. Cover with a clean, dry cloth and let rest 10 minutes so the gluten strands relax and the dough will be easier to roll out.

On a lightly floured countertop, pat one portion of the dough into a fat rectangle and sprinkle lightly with flour. With a floured rolling pin, roll half of dough into a rectangle about 14 × 18 inches—you may need to re-flour the counter and/or the surface of the dough as you work. Spread dough with half of the melted butter and sprinkle on half of the cinnamon sugar filling, leaving a ½-inch border of "clean dough" on the top edge. Brush a little water on that top edge.

Starting with the shorter edge, roll dough up tightly and pinch to seal the seam. Using a sharp knife, cut into six equal slices and place them cut side up, evenly spaced in half of a lightly greased 13 × 9 inch cake pan. Repeat with second portion of dough. Cover with a clean, dry towel and let rise until nearly doubled, 30 to 45 minutes. Bake in preheated 350°F oven on the middle rack for 25 to 30 minutes. The interior temperature of the rolls should be 190°F to 195°F. Cool in the pan on a wire rack. Drizzle on icing (see page 79) and serve while still warm.

Don't be too worried about laying the rolls in perfectly straight rows in the pan. They will self adjust as they rise.

NOTES

— If you have a little trouble getting a perfect rectangle of rolled out dough, you may need to trim a narrow strip from the sides of the dough to make straighter edges. Don't be too upset about this—I have to do it all the time!

— Here is a simple icing recipe: In a small microwave-safe bowl, mix 3 Tbs. of milk with 1 cup of powdered sugar and 1 tsp. of vanilla and whisk with a fork until smooth. Add more milk as needed to reach the consistency of icing you want. Heat in microwave on high for 30 seconds and drizzle or brush on rolls while still warm.

— The butter and brown sugar in the filling turn into a light caramel on the interior of these rolls, so they need only light frosting.

— These are sizable rolls, so be sure to use a pan that is at least 2 inches deep or you might find the rolls rising right out of the pan!

Photo Not Available

My apologies. I intended to show you a photo of a finished cinnamon roll covered in icing, but I couldn't keep one on the abbey table long enough to take the picture!

Butterfly Breakfast Rolls

1 batch of Basic Sweet Dough, risen once (page 68)
2 12-oz. cans of cake and pastry filling, any flavor

Punch down dough and knead lightly to expel larger air bubbles; divide dough into two portions. Cover with a clean, dry cloth and let rest 10 minutes to allow the gluten strands to relax so it will be easier to roll out.

On a lightly floured countertop, pat one portion of the dough into a fat rectangle and sprinkle lightly with flour. With a floured rolling pin, roll the portion of dough into a 12 × 18 inch rectangle. Spread with filling. Starting from the long edge, roll dough up jelly-roll fashion and pinch seam to seal.

Using a sharp knife, cut the roll into 9 wedges (see illustration). Turn each wedge short side up and press the handle of a wooden spoon across each—this presses the dough out to form the "wings."

Place rolls about two inches apart on a lightly greased baking sheet. Repeat with second portion of dough. Cover the baking pans with clean, dry cloths and let rise 30 to 45 minutes or until doubled.

Bake in a preheated 350°F oven for 15 to 20 minutes or until lightly browned. Remove rolls from pan and cool on wire racks.

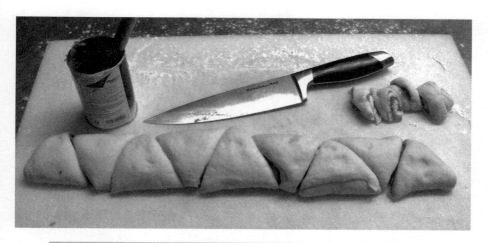

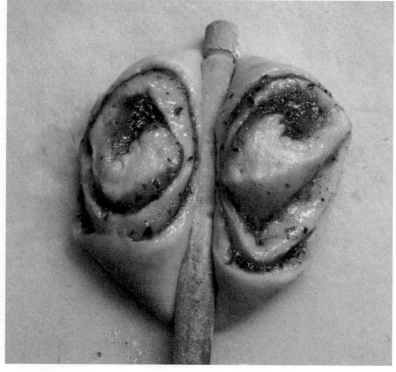

NOTES

— If you use almond filling, the rolls will be sweet enough, and you won't need to frost them. Try apricot filling and then make a light frosting flavored with orange zest to drizzle over the top (see page 79 for basic icing recipe), or use the cinnamon sugar filling on page 77 and make a light glaze by mixing powdered sugar with hazelnut-flavored half and half.

— You could make just nine rolls and use the remainder of the dough for one of the other recipes in this section. For weekend guests, make the butterflies for breakfast and crescent rolls for dinner—you'll be a hit!

Rose Rolls

You'll look like a professional pastry chef with these unique dinner rolls shaped like roses. Just as easy to shape as cinnamon rolls and truly beautiful on the dinner table. Makes 12 rolls.

½ batch of Basic Sweet Dough, risen once (page 68)
2 Tbs. butter, melted

Punch dough down and knead lightly to expel larger air bubbles. Cover with a clean, dry cloth and let rest 10 minutes to allow the gluten strands to relax so it will be easier to roll out. On a lightly floured board, roll dough out into a rectangle 12 inches long by 15 inches wide. Brush the dough with the melted butter, leaving ½ inch of the top edge dry. Roll the dough up jelly-roll style. Lightly brush the top edge with a little water, so it will stick to the roll; pinch to seal.

Using a sharp knife, cut the roll into 12 even pieces. Cut side down, place them into the cups of a lightly greased muffin tin. Using a pair of scissors, cut an "X" in the top of each roll—you should cut about ⅔ of the way through the roll (see next page). Cover and let rise in a warm place until doubled, 30 to 45 minutes. Bake in a preheated 375°F oven for 10 to 12 minutes, or until lightly browned. Remove from pans and place on wire racks to cool slightly. If desired, brush tops of rolls with more melted butter before serving warm.

NOTES

— The size of the cups for muffin tins can vary greatly, and you want to use the deepest ones you can find—but not those giant "Texas size" muffin tins! You'll know if yours are too small if the cut rolls don't quite fit into the cups. You can adapt by rolling the dough a bit wider to start.

— You can make these as cinnamon rolls and then add a little red food coloring to your icing to make pink breakfast roses. One of my friends made them for his girlfriend for Valentine's Day. What could be sweeter than a dozen edible roses, homemade with love?

Final Exam

Well, Breadheads, now that we have arrived at the end of the course, your professor has a confession to make.

I am not America's foremost authority on bread baking.

You probably already knew that, but I wanted full disclosure here. The cookbooks I write are not particularly complex or profound. I don't teach people how to make exquisite artisan breads using Old World techniques paired with the most up-to-date culinary science. For that, you need Peter Reinhart's *The Bread Baker's Apprentice* (Ten Speed Press, 2001). There are plenty of ethnic breads I've never even seen and can't advise you on how to make them. But Christine Ingram and Jennie Shapter can, which is why they wrote *The Best Ever Book of Bread* (Metro Books, 2010), a cookbook that educates and inspires me every time I open it. I compare my slim volumes to Bernard Clayton's *New Complete Book of Breads* (300 recipes, 748 pages; Simon & Schuster, 2003) and realize that if you removed all the hardback covers, the stack of my complete works would come up short by comparison.

So my niche in the world of bread cookbooks is to help people to learn how to bake bread the way their grandmothers did—nothing too fancy at first, with a lot of emphasis (as you may have noticed) on baking for family meals and celebrations with friends. I like to provide traditional recipes, traditional methods, and a few shortcuts and tricks along the way. Above all, I want to pass along not just recipes but *reasons* to bake: the urge to create, the desire to nourish body and soul, the basic human need to *connect* with other people in a world that increasingly isolates us and drives us apart.

So I keep writing bread books, in part because I belong to an abbey with an aging and shrinking population, and somebody has to pay for health care. I write because not every aspiring baker has the time and patience for an artisan bread recipe that takes nine hours to complete, regardless of the perfection of the crust and the complexity of the flavors. I write because people taste my honey oatmeal bread and ask for the recipe, then later tell me it has become a family favorite. And I write because when I take Pull Apart Garlic Bread out of the oven, fragrant with butter and herbs and real Pecorino Romano, I can't imagine not wanting to share. I'm grateful that other bakers feel the same way, so that I can keep learning, too. I know what I know because Peter and Bernard, Beth Hensperger and Rose Levy Beranbaum, and James Beard and my mom all know more than I do. And I can say that without resentment or envy or bitterness, with genuine gratitude.

So class, there is no final exam. (Pause for cheers of surprise and delight.) If by now you've learned anything at all from my example, you'll realize that Breadhead University may give you a diploma, but you'll never really graduate. If you've become a true Breadhead, you'll keep buying cookbooks and actually *use* them to *bake* things. You'll begin a search for the perfect stoneware crock, like the one your aunt used to make raisin bread. You'll ruthlessly throw out any number of unused appliances and pots to make room for an ever-growing collection of baking pans. You will never stop learning new things about baking bread—and your family and friends will be eternally grateful.

God bless and happy baking—class dismissed!